# Fiddle Time Christmas

## A stockingful of 32 easy pieces for violin

### Kathy and David Blackwell

illustrations by John Eastwood

Welcome to **Fiddle Time Christmas.** You'll find:

- 32 great Christmas tunes—carols and pieces
- all the well-known favourites, plus some less familiar gems
- includes words to sing along
- solos and duets
- easy chord symbols for guitar or keyboard accompaniment
- finger patterns 0-1-23 and 0-12-3

MUSIC DEPARTMENT

OXFORD
UNIVERSITY PRESS

# OXFORD
### UNIVERSITY PRESS

Great Clarendon Street, Oxford OX2 6DP, England
198 Madison Avenue, New York, NY10016, USA

Oxford University Press is a department of the University of Oxford.
It furthers the University's aim of excellence in research, scholarship,
and education by publishing worldwide

Oxford is a registered trade mark of Oxford University Press
in the UK and in certain other countries

1 3 5 7 9 10 8 6 4 2

ISBN 0–19–322090–3

Music and text origination by
Barnes Music Engraving Ltd., East Sussex
Printed in Great Britain on acid-free paper by
Halstan & Co. Ltd., Amersham, Bucks.

# Contents

# Hark! the herald-angels sing

Felix Mendelssohn (1809–47)

Hark! the he - rald - an - gels sing_ Glo - ry to the new-born King; Peace on earth and

mer - cy mild,_ God and sin - ners re - con-ciled: Joy-ful all ye na-tions rise,_

Join the tri - umph of the skies, With the'an-gel - ic host pro-claim, Christ is_ born in

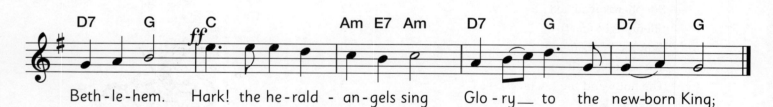

Beth - le - hem. Hark! the he - rald - an - gels sing Glo - ry_ to the new-born King;

# Mary had a baby

American trad.

Ma-ry had a ba - by, Yes, Lord! Ma-ry had a ba - by, Yes, my Lord!

Ma-ry had a ba - by, Yes, Lord! Peo-ple keep a-com-in', and the train done gone!

# The holly and the ivy

English trad.

**Brightly**

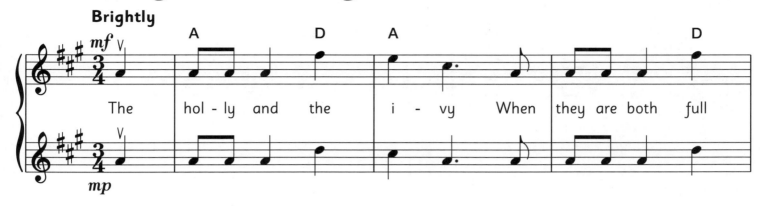

The hol - ly and the i - vy When they are both full

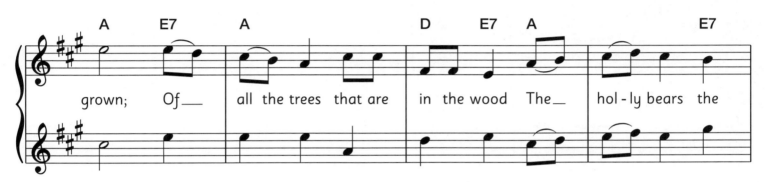

grown; Of__ all the trees that are in the wood The__ hol - ly bears the

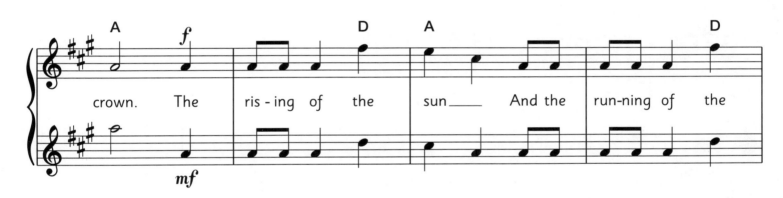

crown. The ris - ing of the sun___ And the run-ning of the

deer, The__ play-ing of the mer-ry or - gan, Sweet sing-ing in the choir.

# Ding dong! merrily on high

16th-century French melody

**Cheerfully**

Ding dong! mer-ri-ly on high in heav'n the bells are ring - ing:
Ding dong! ve-ri-ly the sky is riv'n with an - gel sing - ing.

Glo - - - - - - - -

- - - ri - a, Ho - san - na in ex - cel - sis!

# Andrew mine, Jasper mine

Moravian carol

**Fairly quick**

An - drew mine, Jas - per mine, Ti - mo - thy and A - bel,

Hur - ry to Beth - le - hem, to the com - mon sta - ble.

There you'll find a ba - by small, sleep - ing in a swad - dling shawl;

On your way, on your way, to our Sa - viour born to - day.

# Silent night

Franz Gruber (1787–1863)

Tenderly

Si - lent night, ho - ly night, All is calm,

all is bright; Round yon vir - gin mo - ther and child.

Ho - ly in - fant so ten - der and mild, Sleep in

hea - ven-ly peace,___ Sleep___ in hea - ven-ly peace.

# I saw three ships

English trad.

**Like a dance**

I saw three ships come sailing in On Christmas Day, on Christmas Day, I

saw three ships come sailing in On Christmas Day in the morning.

# O little town of Bethlehem

English trad.

O little town of Bethlehem, How still we see thee lie!
Above thy deep and dreamless sleep The silent stars go by.

Yet in thy dark streets shineth The everlasting light; The

hopes and fears of all the years Are met in thee tonight.

# Christmas Calypso

**Happy**

So dance the Christ-mas Ca-lyp-so in the sun,—

Je-sus is born for ev-'ry-one;— Sing out with joy and

**Fine**

stamp your feet,— move to the ca-lyp-so beat!—

*mf*

Way back in Beth-le-hem, in a sim-ple sta-ble,

**D.%. al Fine**

Je-sus, that ba-by boy,— came to save us all! So dance the

# Once in Royal David's city

H. J. Gauntlett (1805–76)

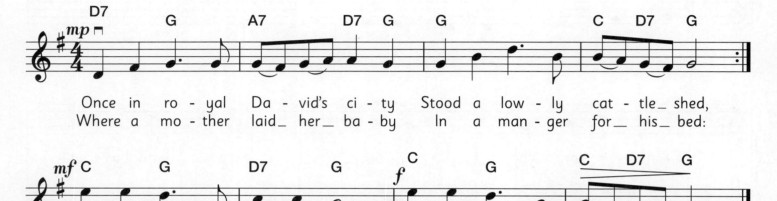

Once in ro - yal Da - vid's ci - ty Stood a low - ly cat - tle_ shed,
Where a mo - ther laid_ her_ ba - by In a man - ger for_ his_ bed:

Ma - ry was that mo - ther mild, Je - sus Christ her lit - tle_ child.

# Go tell it on the mountain

American trad.

**With energy**

Go tell it on the moun - tain, o - ver the hills and ev - 'ry - where;

Go tell it on the moun - tain that Je - sus Christ is born!

Shep-herds kept their watch-ing o'er wand-'ring flocks by night; Be -

- hold from out of hea - ven there shone a ho - ly light:____

10

# O Christmas tree

German trad.

# We wish you a merry Christmas

trad. West Country

We wish you a mer-ry Christ-mas, We wish you a mer-ry Christ-mas, We

wish you a mer-ry Christ-mas And a hap-py New Year. Good

tid-ings we bring To you and your kin; We

wish you a mer-ry Christ-mas And a hap-py New Year.

## Shepherds watched

Czech carol

Shep-herds watched their lambs and sheep, Through the night so dark and deep.

Lo, the an-gel in the skies, Bid-ding them to stand and rise.

Hi-dom, hi-dom, hi-do-dom, Hi-dom, hi-dom, hi-do-dom.

Hi-dom, hi-dom, hi-do-dom, Hi-dom, hi-dom, hi-do-dom.

# We three kings

J. H. Hopkins (1820–91)

We three kings of O - ri - ent are; Bear - ing gifts we

tra - verse a - far Field and foun - tain, moor and moun - tain,

Fol - low - ing yon - der star: O____ star of won - der,

star of night, Star with roy - al beau - ty bright, West - ward

lead - ing, still pro - ceed - ing, Guide us to thy per - fect light.

# O come, all ye faithful

J. F. Wade (*c.*1711–86)

# Bethl'em lay a-sleeping

Polish carol

Beth-l'em lay a-sleep-ing, long, so long a-go, Twink-ling stars were peep-ing, long, so long a-go, When to earth a ba-by came the lit-tle Je-sus was his name, So long, long a-go.

# Good King Wenceslas

*Piae Cantiones* (1582)

Good King Wen-ces-las look'd out On the Feast of Ste-phen,
When the snow lay round a-bout, Deep, and crisp, and ev-en:
Bright-ly shone the moon that night, Though the frost was cru-el,
When a poor man came in sight, Ga-th'ring win-ter fu-el.

## Deck the hall

Welsh trad.

Deck the hall with boughs of hol - ly, Fa la la la la, fa la la la;

'Tis the sea - son to be jol - ly, Fa la la la la, fa la la la.

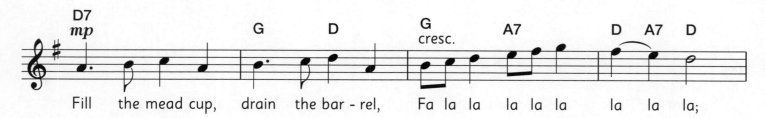

Fill the mead cup, drain the bar - rel, Fa la la la la la la la la;

Troll the an - cient Christ-mas ca - rol, Fa la la la la, fa la la la.

16

# Away in a manger

William J. Kirkpatrick (1838–1921)

# The first Nowell

English trad.

# Zither Carol

**Brightly**

Girls and boys, leave your toys, make no noise, Kneel at his crib and wor-ship him.

At thy shrine, child di-vine, we are thine, Our Sa-viour's here.

'Hal-le-lu-jah' the church bells ring, 'Hal-le-lu-jah' the an-gels sing,

'Hal-le-lu-jah' from ev-'ry-thing. All must draw near.

# God rest you merry, gentlemen

English trad.

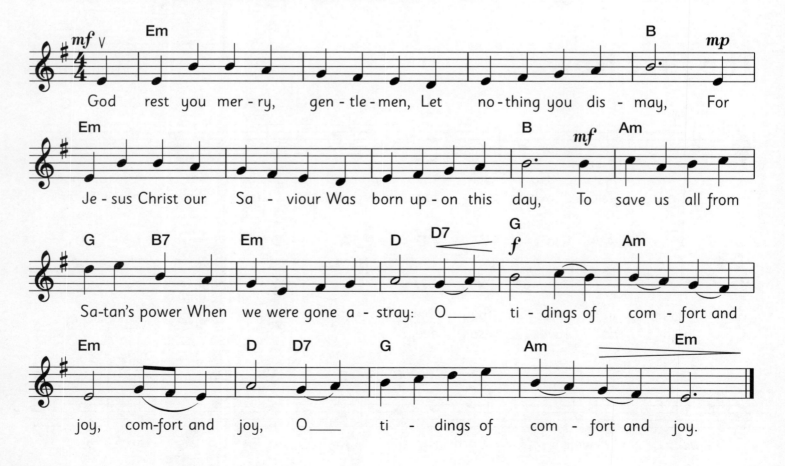

God rest you mer-ry, gen-tle-men, Let no-thing you dis-may, For

Je-sus Christ our Sa - viour Was born up-on this day, To save us all from

Sa-tan's power When we were gone a - stray: O___ ti - dings of com - fort and

joy, com-fort and joy, O___ ti - dings of com - fort and joy.

18

# While shepherds watched their flocks

*Este's Psalter* (1592)

While shep-herds watched their flocks by night, All seat-ed on the ground, The an - gel of the Lord came down, And glo - ry shone a - round.

# Children, go!

Spiritual

**Lively**

Child - ren, go where I send thee! How shall I send thee? I'm gon-na send thee one by one, One for the lit-tle bit-ty ba - by boy, Born, born, born in Beth-le - hem.

# Skaters' Waltz

Emil Waldteufel (1837–1915)

# Dance of the Reed Pipes

(from the *Nutcracker* ballet)

Pyotr Ilyich Tchaikovsky (1840–93)

# Jingle, bells

J. Pierpont (1822–93)

**Happily**

Jin-gle, bells, jin-gle, bells, jin-gle all the way; Oh, what fun it

is to ride in a one-horse o-pen sleigh!__ Jin-gle, bells, jin-gle, bells,

jin-gle all the way; Oh, what fun it is to ride in a one-horse o-pen sleigh!

# Infant holy, infant lowly

Polish carol

**Like a lullaby**

In-fant ho - ly, In-fant low - ly, For his bed a cat-tle stall;
Ox-en low - ing, Lit-tle know - ing Christ the Babe is Lord of all.

Swift are wing - ing, An-gels sing - ing, No-wells ring - ing, Ti-dings, bring - ing,

Christ the Babe is Lord of all, Christ the Babe is Lord of all.

# Child in a manger

Celtic trad.

Child in a man - ger, Je - sus our Sa - viour,

Born of a vir - gin ho - ly and mild;

Sent from the high - est, Come down in glo - ry;

Tell the glad sto - ry, Wel-come the child.

# Hogmanay Reel

# Auld Lang Syne

Scottish trad.

Should auld ac-quain-tance be for-got, and_ nev - er brought to mind? Should

auld ac-quain-tance be for-got, for the sake of auld lang syne? For

auld___ lang___ syne, my dear, for auld___ lang___ syne; We'll

tak' a cup o' kind - ness yet, for the sake of auld lang syne.